ALL ABOUT ANCIENT PEOPLES

THE EGYPTIANS

Anita Ganeri

STARGAZER BOOKS
Mankato, Minnesota

How to use this book

The key below shows the separate subject areas in this book. It includes information about language and literature, science and math, history, geography, and the Arts.

Introduction

The Ancient Egyptian civilization was one of the oldest and greatest in the world. Countless tombs and temples have been excavated to give us an insight into the splendor of Ancient Egypt and its wonderful treasures. Egyptian learning, architecture, and even their gods can all be detected in later civilizations, such as those of Greece and Rome.

© Aladdin Books Ltd 2010

Created and produced by
Aladdin Books Ltd

First published in 2010
by Stargazer Books,
distributed by
Black Rabbit Books
P.O. Box 3263
Mankato, MN 56002

Printed in the United States

The author, Anita Ganeri, M.A., has written many books for children on history, natural history, and other topics.

The historical consultant, Dr. Anne Millard, has written many books for children on history and archaeology.

Library of Congress Cataloging-in-Publication Data

Ganeri, Anita, 1961-
  The Egyptians / Anita Ganeri.
    p. cm. -- (All about ancient peoples)
  Includes index.
  ISBN 978-1-59604-203-2
  1. Egypt--Civilization--To 332 B.C.--Juvenile literature. I.
Title.
  DT61.G334 2009
  932--dc22

              2008016505

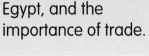

Geography

The symbol of the planet Earth shows where geographical facts are included. These sections look at the mineral resources of Ancient Egypt, and the importance of trade.

Language and literature

An open book is the sign for information on language. These sections explore the myths and legends in Ancient Egypt surrounding death and the afterlife. They also look at the effect of Egyptian culture on writers.

Science and math

The microscope symbol indicates where a science or math subject is included. The intriguing process of mummification is just one of the topics looked at in these sections.

History

The sign of the scroll and the hourglass indicates where historical information is given. These sections look at events in the history of Ancient Egypt and examine the impact on our society today.

Social history

The symbol of a family shows where information about social history is given. These sections aim to provide an insight into the everyday lives of the Ancient Egyptians.

Arts, crafts, and music

This symbol indicates where information on arts, crafts, or music is included. Activities involve writing out a message using Ancient Egyptian hieroglyphics.

Contents

The Land of Egypt

More than 7,000 years ago, one of the world's first and greatest civilizations grew up along the banks of the Nile River in Egypt. The earliest villages were formed by hunters driven east by drought from the grasslands of central Africa. In time, the villagers formed two kingdoms—Lower Egypt in the Nile Delta and Upper Egypt in the valley. In about 3100 BC, King Menes united the country and built his capital at Memphis. He also established the first Egyptian Dynasty, known as Dynasty I.

Rosetta

Alexandria

Pyramids and Sphinx at Giza

Giza

Bast

Statue of Ramses II at Memphis

Memphis

Step pyramid at Saqqara

El Faiyum

Bent pyramid at Maidum

Bahriya Oasis

Beni Hassan

Rock tombs at Beni Hassan

El Amama

WESTERN DESERT

Osiris

Akhenatan at El Amama

Hathor temple at Dendera

Abydos

Dendera

Dakhla Oasis

Colossi of Memnon in Valley of the Kings

RED SEA

Kharga Oasis

Temple at Thebes

Aswan

Red Crown of Lower Egypt

White Crown of Upper Egypt

Temple on island of Philae

Tomb of Ramses II at Abu Simbel

Abu Simbel

Wadi Halfa

NUBIA

Fort at Buhen

The desert

For the Ancient Egyptians, the Red Land, or desert, was a dangerous and sinister place. It was largely uncultivated and desolate, with a few fertile spots, called oases. Oases were places where underground water seeped to the surface.

Natural resources

The rich, black, silty soil of the Nile was Ancient Egypt's greatest natural resource, but not its only one. Large amounts of limestone, sandstone, and granite were quarried from the desert hills above the Nile, and used for building and sculpting. The deserts also contained rich supplies of gold, copper, and semiprecious stones, such as amethysts, garnets, and feldspars.

Granite statue of Ramses II

The Inundation

Every year the Nile River flooded and deposited fertile, black soil on both banks. This was known as the Inundation. It was caused by melting snow and rainwater from the mountains in Ethiopia swelling the river. This water reached Egypt in June or July. When the flood waters subsided, the Egyptians were left with soil that was ideal for farming. The Ancient Egyptians called the fertile land *Kemet*, which means "Black Land."

Double Crown of the united Egypt

King Menes

When King Menes united Egypt he took the official title of "King of Upper and Lower Egypt." The two royal crowns (far *left*), were combined at this time to form the Double Crown (*above*).

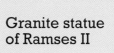

A colorful legacy

Egyptian culture is still represented in musicals like *Joseph and His Amazing Technicolor Dreamcoat*. The tale is based on a Bible story about a boy who was sold into slavery in Egypt and ended up giving advice to the Pharaoh.

The Old Kingdom

The Old Kingdom began in 2686 BC with Dynasty III. This was one of the greatest periods in Egyptian history. The country was ruled by a strong government and extended its trading links with Nubia and lands around the Red Sea and the Mediterranean. Art, culture, and scholarship also flourished. The Old Kingdom was the great age of pyramid building.

Date chart

c.5000–3100 BC
Predynastic Period
• c.3100 BC King Menes unites Egypt.

LOWER EGYPT

Giza
Saqqara — Memphis

Hierakonopolis

Abydos

UPPER EGYPT

Aswan

1st Cataract

TRADE AND RAIDS

NUBIA

2nd Cataract

c.3100–2686 BC
Archaic Period
Dynasties I and II
c.2686–2150 BC
The Old Kingdom
Dynasties III and IV
• c.2686–2613 BC
Dynasty III
Reign of King Zoser
• c.2589–2566 BC
Dynasty IV
Reign of King Khufu
• c.2580 BC
Building of the Great Pyramid of Khufu at Giza
• c.2494–2345 BC
Dynasty V
Kings devoted to the sun god, Re, and take the title "Son of Re"
• c.2246–2150 BC
Dynasty VI
Reign of King Pepi II; the longest recorded reign in history.
c.2150–2040 BC
First Intermediate Period
Dynasties VII–X

King Menkaure and his queen

Ancient Egypt was ruled by kings, believed to be the god Horus in human form. From about 1554 BC, the king was also called Pharaoh, from the Egyptian words *per aa*, meaning "palace." The position of king was inherited and passed to the eldest son. To keep the blood pure the king often married a close relation.

The administration

The king appointed officials called viziers to help him rule. They acted for the king in all matters of government and the administration of justice. Ancient Egypt was divided into 42 districts, called nomes. Each nome was governed on behalf of the king by an official called a nomarch.

Taxes were paid according to a person's profession. Farmers paid their taxes in crops, while skilled workers were taxed on the goods or services they provided.

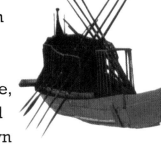

Actual boats have been found in a number of tombs around the pyramids of Giza. They were probably used by the king in life, and also to carry him to his final resting place. The boat shown right belonged to King Khufu. It can be seen today at Giza.

The Sphinx

The three great pyramids at Giza (left) were built about 4,500 years ago. They were tombs for the Kings Khufu, Khafre, and Menkaure. The pyramids are guarded by a huge stone statue, called a sphinx. It has the body of a lion and a human head whose features are thought to be those of King Khafre.

King Radjedef (*above left*) followed his father, King Khufu, to the throne.

Trade with Nubia

The country of Nubia lay to the south of Egypt. It was considered so important for trade that the Egyptians cut a canal through the First Cataract (a place where rocks blocked the Nile River), to speed up the journey to Nubia. The Egyptians bought leopard skins, ivory, ebony, slaves, and later gold from Nubia in exchange for luxury goods.

The Pyramid Complex

The Great Pyramid of Giza, built for King Khufu, was one of the Seven Wonders of the ancient world. The pyramids are still among the greatest engineering feats ever known. They were built as permanent tombs for the kings. The first pyramids had stepped sides so that the king's soul could climb up to reach heaven. The later ones were built with straight sides to represent the sun's rays.

Stone quarries

Vast amounts of stone were needed to build the pyramids. Stone from quarries nearby was hauled to the sites on sledges. Limestone from Tura and granite from Aswan were brought down the Nile by barge.

The king's body was brought by river and prepared for burial in the Valley Temple. Then it was carried down the causeway to the Mortuary Temple.

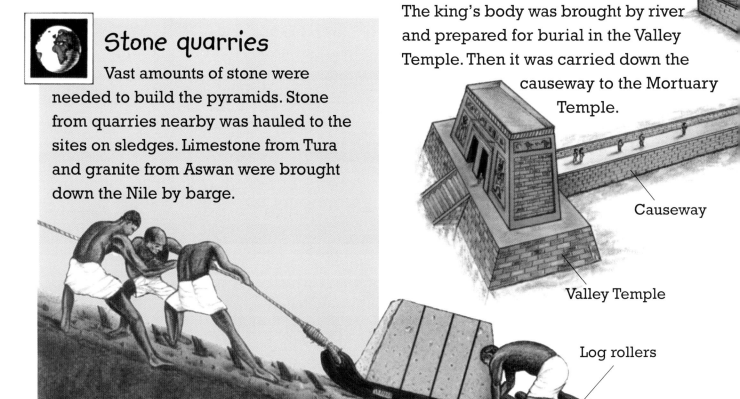

Causeway

Valley Temple

Log rollers

Wooden sledge

Measuring

The pyramids required a lot of planning. First, the base was marked out to form a perfect square. Using modern equipment, experts have found that the Egyptians' measurements were so accurate that one corner of the Great Pyramid is only 0.4 in (1 cm) higher than the other.

Water trenches, measuring rods, and string were used to make sure the pyramids' foundations were level (*right*).

The accuracy of pyramid angles may have been achieved by counting the revolutions of a rolling drum (*left*).

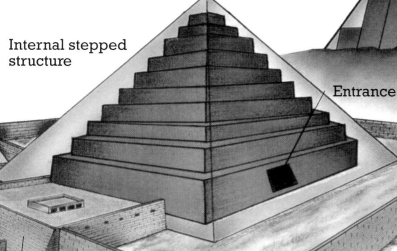

Inside a pyramid
1. Entrance
2. Ascending corridor
3. Grand gallery
4. Pharaoh's chamber
5. Air shafts
6. Burial chambers
7. Escape shaft
8. Descending corridor

Internal stepped structure

Entrance

Temenos wall

Mortuary Temple

Pyramid building

The Ancient Egyptians had no cranes, trucks, or mechanized building equipment. Teams of workers dragged the huge stone blocks into position using wooden sledges, which they hauled up a mud and brick ramp. As the pyramid grew, the ramp grew longer. When all the layers were in place, the capstone (topmost stone) was added. Then the whole pyramid was covered in limestone casing blocks. Most of the people who worked on the pyramids were ordinary farmers.

The one that went wrong

The core of the Maidum Pyramid (*below*) rises up from a pile of debris. It is all that is left of an early failed attempt at a true pyramid. It was originally a seven-stepped structure, but it did not have proper foundations and, as a result, it collapsed.

Mexican pyramids

From the 13th to 15th century AD, the Aztecs of Mexico built their own pyramids. Temples to their sun god were built on top. A stairway at the front allowed priests to climb up to the temple and offer sacrifices. Amazingly, the Aztecs had never seen, or even heard of, the Egyptian pyramids.

The Middle Kingdom

The Middle Kingdom began in about 2040 BC, when King Mentuhotep II of Dynasty XI reunited Egypt. About 1991 BC, a vizier, Amenemhat, seized the throne. Under his rule and that of his heirs (Dynasty XII), Egypt became wealthy and powerful once more. Following a series of weak rulers during Dynasty XIII, Egypt was overrun by the Hyksos people from Asia, leading to one of the darkest periods in Egypt's history.

Date chart

c.2040–1640 BC
The Middle Kingdom
• c.2040 BC
Dynasty XI
Mentuhotep II overthrows his rivals and reunites Egypt.
  • c.1991–1783 BC
  Dynasty XII
  Egypt conquers Nubia and builds a string of forts on the Second Cataract.

Cedar wood trade

• c.1991–1962 BC
Dynasty XII
Reign of Amenemhat I
• c.1787–1783 BC
Dynasty XII
Reign of Princess Sobek Neferu as "King"
• c.1786–1640 BC
Dynasty XIII
Hyksos overrun Egypt.
c. 1640–1552 BC
The Second Intermediate Period

Hyksos invasion

Copper and turquoise

Amethyst

Copper

Gold mines

KEY
○ Mines
▓ Forts

During the Middle Kingdom, the Egyptians conquered Nubia and traded far and wide. Traders brought rare and valuable goods to Egypt and increased the country's wealth. Gold came from the Nubian Desert, and cedar and cypress wood from Syria and Lebanon. Merchants did not use money—they bartered with other goods or *deben* (see page 31).

Art by design

Egyptian works of art were governed by strict rules. The artists first applied a layer of plaster to the wall to make it level. Then they marked out a grid to help them get the drawings in proportion. Their sketches were corrected by a supervisor, then they filled in details and color. Important people, such as Pharaohs, were represented by large figures. The human figure was usually drawn in profile, though with a full view of the eyebrow and eye.

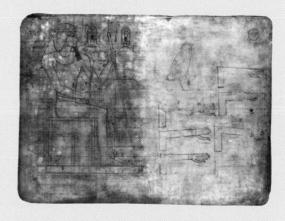

The figures are usually acting out myths, rituals, and historical events.

The engraving on the left shows a procession of armed attendants. Each Egyptian had a shield decorated with an individual design. This meant he was able to recognize his own shield when called to battle. Military equipment was often included in tombs as a symbol of protection in the afterworld.

Egyptian soldiers used spears, axes, swords, bows and arrows, and maces. These were usually made out of wood and bronze. They carried ox-hide shields. From the New Kingdom onward, they wore armor made out of leather strips.

Chariot charge

The Hyksos army used horse-drawn chariots and improved bows to help them defeat the Egyptians. These had never been seen in Egypt before. By the time of the New Kingdom, they had become an important part of the Egyptian army. By learning to use the chariots and weapons of their enemies, they succeeded in driving the invaders out. The Pharaoh became the Commander-in-Chief. The army divisions were named after gods, such as Amun and Re.

A New Kingdom chariot

Language and Writing

The Ancient Egyptians spoke a language related to the languages of the Middle East and North Africa. Those who could write used a system of picture writing called hieroglyphics. The Egyptians started to use hieroglyphics in about 3000 BC. Each picture could stand for an object and a sound.

Ink blocks

Reed pens

A scribe

Breaking the code

Hieroglyphics were last used in about 394 AD. For more than 1,400 years, no one could read or understand them. In 1799, however, a soldier in Napoleon Bonaparte's army in Egypt found a large, stone slab— the Rosetta Stone.

On this stone was a text carved by Egyptian priests in 196 BC to mark the crowning of King Ptolemy V. The same text was copied in Ancient Egyptian hieroglyphics, demotic script, and Greek. By comparing these three, a French scholar called François Champollion was finally able to crack the code in 1822.

Champollion

The Rosetta Stone

Writing hieroglyphics

The word *hieroglyph* is Greek for sacred carvings. Egyptian hieroglyphs were usually written or carved by highly trained men called scribes. Scribes were very important as the Egyptians loved to keep records. Use the symbols below to write your own hieroglyphic message.

*   i   y   y   y   *   w   *   b   p   f

Papyrus paper

The Egyptians wrote on a paper-like material called papyrus. Papyrus was made from pith taken from reeds and covered in linen after several processes. Sheets of papyrus were often fixed together to form a roll.

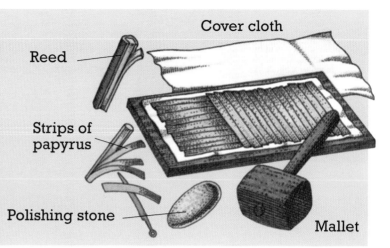

Cover cloth

Reed

Strips of papyrus

Polishing stone

Mallet

Hieroglyphs

For daily use, two simpler forms of shorthand script were created. Hieratic script (*left*) was used in the Old Kingdom. By 700 BC, demotic script was in use.

Hieroglyphs were not used in everyday life. They were reserved for important inscriptions, such as those on tombs or temples and for affairs of state.

B

B

There were many different ways of writing hieroglyphs. From left to right, right to left, or top to bottom. If an animal faced right (A), you read from right to left. If it faced left (B), you read from left to right.

A

A

The name or symbol of a ruler appeared in hieroglyphs within an oval frame called a cartouche (*left*).

P O L Y S
T O M Y S

K L I O P A D R A

Champollion solved the riddle of the Rosetta Stone using names like Ptolemy and Cleopatra (*left* and *above*). See if you can spot which letters appear in both names.

* No translation

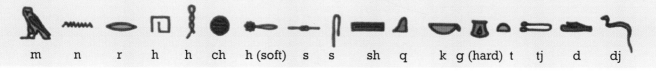

| m | n | r | h | h | ch | h (soft) | s | s | sh | q | k | g (hard) | t | tj | d | dj |

The New Kingdom

The New Kingdom began in 1552 BC and saw Egypt build a huge empire. The Hyksos were driven out and the Pharaoh himself took control of the army. By the time of Tuthmosis III (c.1479–1425 BC), Egypt had become the greatest power in the Middle East.

At least two queens seized the throne during the New Kingdom. The greatest queen was Hatshepsut (1473–1458 BC). She married her half-brother, Tuthmosis II. When he died, she became "King." She was always addressed as "His Majesty." One of her greatest achievements was to send a fleet of ships to the land of Punt, a strange place on the east coast of Africa. No one from Egypt had been there for over 200 years. The expedition brought back myrhh for making the incense used in temples.

Ramses II in his Blue or War Crown

Boat building

Boats were the main form of transportation in Ancient Egypt. The earliest ones were made from reeds and were rowed. Sails were soon invented and wood gradually replaced the reeds. Boats were used for trading at home and abroad, and for funerals.

A trading ship

The greatest discovery

In 1922, British archaeologist Howard Carter discovered the tomb of King Tutankhamun in the Valley of the Kings. The tomb was the only royal tomb of the New Kingdom to be found intact. It was full of wonderful treasures—gold jewelry, statues, furniture, and clothes. The greatest find of all was the mummy of the Pharaoh himself, his face covered by a beautiful gold death mask (*right*).

The temple of Amun-Re at Karnas was extended by Ramses II. He added a great pillared hypostyle, or hall, of 134 painted columns (*see below*). The finished temple was big enough to hold several cathedrals. Ramses also built a spectacular rock-cut temple at Abu Simbel. The temple was guarded by four gigantic statues of the Pharaoh (*see right*), and was designed so that twice a year the rising sun would reach the innermost part and light up the statues of the gods.

The Hypostyle Hall at Karnak

An example of a painted column

c.1552–1085 BC
The New Kingdom
Dynasties XVIII-XX
• c.1552–1305 BC
Dynasty XVIII
• c.1492–1479 BC
Region of Tuthmosis II
• c.1473–1458 BC
Reign of Queen Hatshepsut. Expedition to land of Punt.
• c.1479–1425 BC
Reign of Tuthmosis III. The Egyptian Empire reaches its greatest extent.
• c.1364–1347 BC
Reign of Akhenaten (Amenhotep IV)
• c.1347–1337 BC
Reign of Tutankhamun
• c.1305–1186 BC
Dynasty XIX
• c.1289–1224 BC
Reign of Ramses II
• c.1184–1153 BC
Dynasty XX
Reign of Ramses III
c. 1085–664 BC
The Third
Intermediate Period

Akhenaten

Abu Simbel

An elaborate pendant hung on a string of beads is called a pectoral. The Scarab Pectoral (*above*) was found among the treasures of Tutankhamun's tomb. The boy-king's gold death mask (*left*) was inlaid with semiprecious stones, such as lapis lazuli.

MEDITERRANEAN EMPIRE

Memphis

Egyptian Empire

Thebes

Valley of the Kings

Trade with Punt

The Gods of Egypt

The Ancient Egyptians believed in a large number of gods and goddesses who controlled all aspects of nature and daily life. During the Old and Middle Kingdoms the main god was the sun god, Re. In the New Kingdom, the king of gods was Amun-Re. The main goddess was Isis, the protector of all.

Many of the gods and goddesses were closely related. For example, Re's son, Shu, was god of the air and father of the sky goddess, Nut. She was married to her brother, Geb, the god of Earth. Their son was Osiris. The main gods and goddesses are shown below.

Neith

Re-Harakhte

Ptah of Memphis

Anubis

Sobek

Shu

Horus of Edfu

Isis

Amun of Thebes

Wadjet of Buto

Nekhbet

Ape of Thoth

Akhenaten

Amenhotep IV ruled Ancient Egypt from about 1364 to 1347 BC. He was married to Queen Nefertiti. Amenhotep tried to reform the religion of Ancient Egypt and he is thought to be the first person to worship just one god—the sun god, Aten. In honor of his god, the king changed his name to Akhenaten. However, this reform upset many Egyptians because they wanted to continue to worship many gods. These gods were later restored by Akhenaten's successor, Tutankhamun.

Akhenaten

Temple worship

Ordinary people worshipped the gods at home. The temples were reserved for the priests, priestesses, and the chief priest, the Pharaoh himself. A temple was seen as the god's home on Earth. The god's statue was kept in a shrine deep inside the temple. Each day it was brought out and cleaned, dressed, and offered food and drink. The priestesses said prayers and sang sacred hymns.

Khnum · Thoth · Khonsu · Osiris · Mestert · Hathor with son Ihy · Sekhmet

Lucky charms

Jewelry was worn by everyone in Ancient Egypt. Many pieces bore special symbols that were thought to protect the wearer. These were also worn as amulets or charms. The luckiest amulets were the *ankh* (symbol of life) and *udjat* (eye).

Funerary amulets

Sacred animals

The Ancient Egyptians believed that animals, such as cats, bulls, and birds, were special to certain gods and goddesses. These sacred animals were thought to be chosen by the gods and were therefore treated with the utmost respect. During the Late Period, anyone who killed a cat was sentenced to death. Sacred animals were often mummified.

Sacred scarab amulets

Cats often wore a gold ring to show they were sacred.

Social Structure

Ancient Egyptian society was headed by the Pharaoh. Below him came the royal family and members of the upper classes, including noblemen, landowners, government officials, high-ranking army officials, and priests. Merchants, scribes, craftsmen, soldiers, and sailors made up the middle class. The largest class was the lower class which consisted of peasants and farmers. Below them came the slaves.

Pharaoh

The queen

Nobleman's wife

Priest

Nobleman

Egyptian style

Eyeshadow palette

Both men and women wore make-up and jewelry in Ancient Egypt. To begin their toilet, they would wash with a special paste and water. They used eyeliner, called kohl. Lips and cheeks were painted with red clay (ochre) that was mixed with water. They admired themselves in mirrors and used henna to dye their hair, the soles of their feet, and the palms of their hands. Perfumes were made from scented oils.

Bronze mirror

Jewelry box

Musician

Artist

Statue
of a
servant
girl

The role of women

Some women served as maids to the wives of wealthy nobles. They also worked as nurses, gardeners, weavers, professional mourners, and entertainers. Wealthier women often became priestesses or doctors. Women were also allowed to own property. They could not hold government positions, but could conduct their own court cases.

Women in society

In most ancient societies, women had very few rights. In Egypt it was different; women were respected and had many rights and privileges. In Egyptian art, women have pale skins, suggesting that they spent most of their time indoors. Men are usually shown as being darker-skinned.

Family life

Family life and children were very important to the Ancient Egyptians. They adopted childen if they could not have any of their own. The father was the head of the family, with his eldest son as his heir. Most sons followed their father's profession. Girls learned how to cook, sew, and look after the household.

The engraving (*right*) depicts Nebamun and his wife and daughter hunting in the marshes. The hieroglyphic text refers to "having pleasure, [and] seeing good things . . ."

The Farmer's Year

Farming was the mainstay of Egypt's economy. Most people worked as farmers on large estates. The fertile soil deposited by the Nile each year enabled huge numbers of crops to be grown. The farmers had to pay the landowners by giving them large amounts of their produce as taxes. The crops grown were wheat, barley, flax, dates, grapes, and a large variety of fruit and vegetables.

Irrigation

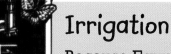

Because Egypt was so hot and dry, irrigation was essential. Canals were dug from the Nile River, and a device called a *shaduf* raised the water to the fields. It had a weight at one end and a bucket on the other.

A shaduf

The farmer's year was split into three seasons—the Inundation (July to November), the Growing season (November to March), and the Harvest (March to July). No work could be done during the Inundation, so many farmers worked on royal buildings to help pay their taxes.

When the floods went down, they plowed the land and sowed the seed. In March, taxmen decided how much produce to take in tax. The wheat could then be harvested.

Tooth trouble

Bread was one of the basic foods in the Egyptian diet. The grain was ground into flour between two stones and sometimes grit got into the bread. Some mummies have teeth worn down by chewing on the gritty bread.

Lavish feasts

Wealthy Egyptians loved to entertain their friends with lavish banquets. The menu might include roast goose or exotic meats, cakes, figs, and plenty of wine. Food was eaten with the fingers. Guests sat with cones of perfumed fat on their heads, which melted when it got too hot to help cool the guests down.

Donkeys carried the wheat to the threshing floor. Cattle were driven across the wheat to separate the grain from the husk. The wheat was then tossed into the air, the husk allowed to blow away, and the grain was put into large baskets.

The calendar

As early as the Old Kingdom, the Ancient Egyptians had devised a 365-day calendar with twelve 30-day months and five additional days. The calendar was based on the flooding of the Nile and the appearance of the star Sirius. The Egyptian calendar has enabled scholars to date much of the history of Egypt and the ancient world. It is also the basis of the calendar we use today.

Grain was stored in large granaries until it was needed. Wheat was ground into flour and used to make bread. Barley was used to make beer. The Egyptians also grew onions, garlic, lettuces, beans, melons, and figs. They raised cattle, sheep, pigs, ducks, geese, and goats. They also kept bees for honey. The Nile provided plenty of fish and wildfowl.

Model of a granary

The engraving (left) shows a scribe counting the geese and eggs, while the herdsmen bow before their master.

The engraving (right) shows fashionable ladies offering each other lotus blooms. Ladies were usually seated apart from the men at banquets.

Egyptians at Home

Egyptian houses varied greatly in size and splendor, depending on the wealth and status of their owners. Houses built in towns were crowded together in narrow streets. Those who could afford it owned a villa in the countryside, with exotic gardens. Poorer families lived in just one room. Cooking was often done outside to reduce a risk of fire. Richer households had many rooms, including servants' quarters.

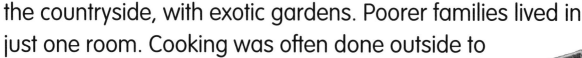

Shrine

Garden

Central hall

Granary court

Kitchen

Servants' quarters

Villas

This is the country villa of a wealthy noble. At the front is a reception area where business was conducted. Behind that is a columned hall where guests would be entertained. The family's private rooms, which included bedrooms and bathrooms, were at the back of the house. Behind them were the kitchen and a grain silo for storing grain to make bread. There were also beautiful gardens, with a pool. It was kept well stocked with fish and lotus flowers. The whole villa was surrounded by a high wall.

Furniture

Egyptian houses were furnished with wooden chairs, beds, chests, and tables. Colorful wall hangings often adorned the walls. The kings and nobles had furniture made of precious ebony or cedar wood, inlaid with gold or precious stones. Chairs were a sign of wealth and high social status. Candles and oil lamps with flax wicks were used for lighting.

Building materials

Temples were meant to last forever, so they were built out of stone. The first houses built were made of reeds. Later houses were built of mud bricks, dried and hardened in the sun. The mud was mixed with grit and straw, shaped, and left to dry. Mud plaster was also used to cover the floor. The finished house was then coated with limestone plaster. Very few Ancient Egyptian houses have survived to the present day.

A model showing brickmakers

Flat roofs for cooking and storage

Cooking was done in a domed oven.

Houses

The houses of poor Egyptians were much smaller and less luxurious than the villa. They had very litle furniture and were usually cramped. On hot nights, people slept on the roof to keep cool. Windows were often small and placed near the ceiling, to avoid the intense sunlight.

Fun and games

Egyptian children loved toys and games like knucklebones and leapfrog. They played with spinning tops, dolls, balls, and wooden animals. The jaw of the wooden lion shown left snaps shut when the string is pulled. One of the most popular board games was called *senet* (shown below). The aim of the game was to reach the kingdom of Osiris, overcoming various evils and obstacles on the way. *Senet* was played with counters, rather like backgammon. Four *senet* boards were found buried with King Tutankhamun.

The magnificent throne of Tutankhamun

A folding stool

Burial Customs

Ancient Egyptians went to great lengths to prepare themselves for death, burial, and the life to come. They believed that a dead person's soul went to an underworld, called *Duat*. Before it reached the next world, the Kingdom of the West, it had to pass many hard tests. Ancient Egyptians believed a person had three souls—the *ka*, the *ba,* and the *akh*. To survive the next world, the body had to be preserved. This led to bodies being mummified.

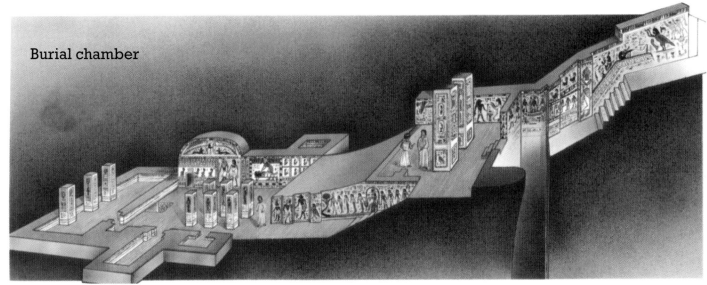

Burial chamber

Tombs of New Kingdom kings were cut deep into the rocks of a valley at Thebes. They had a central tunnel with rooms off, leading to the burial chamber (*see above*).

Model of woman grinding corn

The Egyptians filled their tombs with items they might need in the afterlife—clothes, food, and furniture, for example. Scenes decorated the walls.

Many magical statues of servants, called *shabti*, have been found in the tombs of wealthy Egyptians.

Shabti figure of Amenhotep II

Model of a funerary boat

Poor burials

Very few Egyptians could afford splendid tombs or coffins. Poor people were often buried in simple holes in the hot sand or in a small tomb cut into the ground. Whether rich or poor, all good Egyptians believed Osiris, the Ruler of the Dead, would reward them with a happy eternal life.

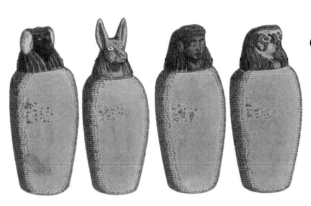
Canopic jars

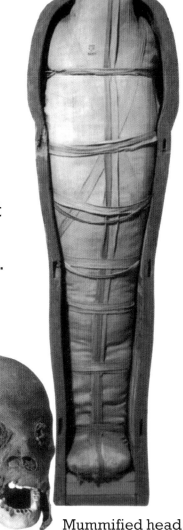

Mummification

Bodies were mummified to stop them rotting. The process was so successful that many have survived to the present day. The first step was to remove the brain, liver, lungs, and intestines. These were stored in special "canopic" jars. The heart was left in place. Then the body was packed in salt to dry it out. The body was padded with cloth to make it look fleshier, then oiled, wrapped in linen, and placed in its coffin. This process took about 70 days.

Mummified head

Funerary texts

Passages of prayers, spells, and hymns were carved on tomb walls. These were intended to guide the dead in the afterlife, to protect them from evil, and to provide for their future needs. The texts were later written down on papyrus scrolls and became known as *The Book of the Dead*. The text and spells were often accompanied by colorful illustrations, such as the one shown below.

In the Judgement Hall, the dead person would stand trial before the god Osiris. The engraving (*right*) shows Anubis—the figure on the left with the head of a jackal—preparing to weigh the dead person's heart against a feather, which was the symbol of truth. If he had led a sinful life, his heart would tip the scales and he would be punished. If he had led a good life, his heart and the feather would balance and he could go on to join his ancestors. The verdict was then recorded by Thoth, the god of wisdom.

Foreign Pharaohs

The end of Dynasty XX signaled the start of Egypt's gradual decline. Egypt had been ruled by a series of foreign kings who came from Libya, Nubia, and Assyria. In 664 BC, Egyptian kings regained power to form Dynasty XXVI. In 525 BC, Egypt was conquered by the Persians, who ruled until 404 BC. Alexander the Great was able to defeat the Persians and made Egypt part of his empire. In 30 BC, Egypt finally fell to the Romans.

Alexander the Great, King of Macedonia and leader of the Greeks, conquered the Persians and arrived in Egypt in 332 BC. When he died in 323 BC, his empire was divided up. His general, Ptolemy, took control of Egypt, eventually declaring himself king. He began the Ptolemaic Dynasty, which ruled Egypt for the next 250 years. Under the early Ptolemies, Egypt flourished, but later rulers caused major unrest.

The Pharos of Alexandria (*right*) is one of the Seven Wonders of the World. Built in 270 BC, it was the world's first lighthouse and stood 400 ft (122 m) high. Its light came from a wood-burning fire in the top.

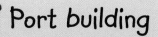

Alexander the Great

Port building

Much of Alexandria—the city Alexander built in 331 BC—was destroyed by earthquakes in the 14th century. The famous lighthouse (*above*), Cleopatra's quarters, and many other buildings collapsed into the sea. Until recently, we only knew of their existence, but two French archaeologists have been unearthing the remains of the sunken part of Alexandria. They believe they have uncovered the foundations of Cleopatra's palace and parts of the lighthouse. This will help us understand how Cleopatra and the citizens of Alexandria lived.

Antony and Cleopatra

Cleopatra VII was the last of the Ptolemaic rulers. With her Roman husband, Mark Antony, she tried to keep Egypt powerful. In 31 BC, however, they were defeated by the Romans at the Battle of Actium. They committed suicide and Egypt became part of the Roman Empire.

The Late Period of Egyptian history lasted from about 664 BC to 332 BC. Egypt recovered some of its power under the Saite kings of Dynasty XXVI. But in 525 BC, King Psamtek III was defeated by the Persian ruler Cambyses, and Egypt became part of the huge Persian Empire.

Influence on art

Under Alexander and the Ptolemaic rulers, Greek art and culture spread to Egypt and began to influence the age-old traditions and conventions of Egyptian art and sculpture. Many of the reliefs carved into the walls of temples during this period show a mixture of Greek and Egyptian styles.

This king's head was carved during the Ptolemaic period.

Date chart

c.1085–664 BC
The Third Intermediate Period
Dynasties XXI–XXV
• c.728–664 BC
Dynasty XXV
Rule of the Nubian kings
c. 664–332 BC
The Late Period
Dynasty XXVI
Rule of the Saite kings
• c.525 BC
The Persians invade Egypt.
• c.404–341 BC
Dynasties XXVIII, XXIX, and XXX
Egypt regains its independence.
• c.341–332 BC
The Persians return and rule Egypt.
332 BC Alexander the Great defeats the Persians and conquers Egypt.
323 BC
Death of Alexander
323–30 BC
The Ptolemies rule Egypt.
• 31 BC
Mark Antony and Cleopatra are defeated by the Roman ruler Octavian at the Battle of Actium.
• 30 BC
Suicide of Mark Antony and Cleopatra. Egypt becomes part of the Roman Empire.
324 AD
Egypt is converted to Christianity.
639–642 AD
The Arabs conquer Egypt and convert many to Islam.

Alexandria

Ptolemaic Empire at its height

The Egyptian Legacy

Since Champollion unlocked the secrets of the Rosetta Stone in 1822, people have marveled at the skills and knowledge of the Ancient Egyptians. They built great cities and monuments—the ones still standing attract millions of visitors each year. They also created exquisite works of art and sculpture. They produced advanced studies of astronomy, mathematics, geography, and medicine. Even though the civilization of Ancient Egypt died out more than 2,000 years ago, its fascination still continues today.

The Nile today

The Nile is the main transportation route of modern Egypt, as it was in the past. Boats called *feluccas* and *dhows* carry goods and passengers. To stop the river flooding, the Aswan High Dam was built between 1960 and 1970 to control the waters of the Nile. Water for irrigation and hydroelectric power now collects in the manmade Lake Nasser behind the dam.

Thousands of people visit Egypt each year, drawn by the grandeur of this ancient civilization.

Some Egyptian monuments, such as the carved stone obelisk shown *top left*, were removed from Egypt during the 19th century. They can now be found in cities throughout the world. The pyramids at Giza (*above*), however, could not be moved, and stand as monuments to a great civilization. Ancient Egyptian influence can also be seen in some modern architecture, such as churches, bridges, and even cemeteries. The building on the *right* in Miami, Florida, reveals the Egyptian influence on the Art Deco movement of the 1920s.

Agriculture today

Up until the 1800s, Egyptian farmers relied upon the yearly Inundation to irrigate their fields and renew the layer of topsoil. Much of Egypt's land is still divided into small fields which are surrounded by irrigation ditches (*see right*). Today the land is irrigated all year round. Dams, canals, and reservoirs were built to trap the water from the Nile. This system was completed when the Aswan Dam was opened in 1968. Today, cotton is Egypt's most valuable crop. Dates, corn, sugar cane, oranges, potatoes, rice, and tomatoes are also grown.

The shaduf used in Ancient Egypt (see page 20) can still be found today in parts of Egypt (right). However, many are now being replaced with electrically driven pumps.

Family planning

Egyptians learned about anatomy from the practice of mummification. This knowledge also helped to influence Greek medicine in the future. The Ancient Egyptians practiced birth control to limit the size of the families. One method involved using honey as a barrier. A far less sweet solution was to use a ball of dung!

c.5000–3100 BC Predynastic Period

Two kingdoms formed—Upper and Lower Egypt. The King of Upper Egypt wore the White Crown and his capital was at Hierakonopolis. The King of Lower Egypt wore the Red Crown. His capital was at Buto.

c.3100–2686 BC Archaic Period

Dynasties I–II Upper and Lower Egypt united by Menes, the first Pharaoh. He built a new capital at Memphis. Royal tombs built near Abydos and Saqqara.

c.2686–2150 BC The Old Kingdom

Dynasties III–VI One of the greatest periods of Egyptian history. The pyramid age.

• 2686–2613 BC Reign of King Zoser
• 2613–2505 BC Reigns of Pharaohs Khufu, Khafre, and Menkaure. Great pyramids and Sphinx built at Giza.

c.2150–2040 BC 1st Intermediate Period *Dynasties VII–X*

Collapse of kings' rule; social and political chaos, wars, and famine.

c.2040–1640 BC Middle Kingdom

Dynasties XI–XIII Egypt reunited by a Prince of Thebes.

c.1640–1552 BC 2nd Intermediate Period *Dynasties XIV–XVII*

Another period of chaos. Invasion by Hyksos who ruled north Egypt.

c.1552–1085 BC The New Kingdom

Dynasties XVIII–XX Hyksos driven out by Pharaoh Ahmose I. Empire expanded by Tuthmosis III. Other significant rulers include Hatshepsut, Amenhotep IV (Akenaton), Tutankhamun, Haremhab, and Ramses II and III.

c.1085–664 BC 3rd Intermediate Period

8000 BC

First hieroglyphs (picture writing) in Egypt c.3500 BC

Old Kingdom in Egypt 2686–2150 BC

Pyramids built in Egypt during Old Kingdom

Egyptian Middle Kingdom 2040–1640 BC

2000 BC

Tutankhamun—the boy pharoah c.1347–1339 BC

New Kingdom in Egypt 1552–1085 BC

Romulus and Remus found the city of Rome 753 BC

500 BC

Beginning of the Roman Empire c.27 BC

Julius Caesar murdered 44 BC

Fall of the Roman Empire AD 476

Viking raids across western Europe AD 793–1000

AD 1000

First Crusade to recapture Holy Land from Muslims AD 1096

First mechanical clock developed AD 1386

The Aztec Empire in Central America AD 1300s–1521

AD c1200–1532 The Inca Empire in South America

8000–5650 BC First cities—
Jericho and Catal Hüyük

3500–3000 BC Wheel
invented by the
Sumerians

Rise of the Indus Valley
civilization 2500–1700 BC

Early Minoan period in
Crete begins c.2500 BC

Stonehenge in England
completed c.1500 BC

c.1766–1122 BC Shang
Dynasty in China

The destruction of Knossos in Crete. End
of the Minoan period c.1400 BC

Birth of Confucius 551 BC

c.500 BC Life of Siddhartha Guatama, the
Buddha

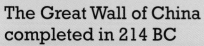

The Golden Age of Greece
479–431 BC

Alexander the Great
conquers Persia, Syria, and
Egypt c.333–330 BC

The Qin Dynasty in
China 221–206 BC

The Great Wall of China
completed in 214 BC

Samurai warriors of Japan
AD 1100s–1850

The plague, or Black Death,
spreads in Europe and Asia
AD 1300s.

First mechanical printing press developed
by Gutenberg in Germany in AD c.1450

Christopher Columbus lands in the
Americas AD 1492.

Glossary

Ankh A lucky amulet which was
the symbol of life.

Cataract A place where the Nile
River was blocked by rocks.

Deben Copper weights used in
trade, instead of money.

Duat The Ancient Egyptian
underworld.

Dynasty A line of kings from
the same family. The dynasties of
Ancient Egypt run from I to XXX.

Hieroglyphics Ancient Egyptian
system of picture writing.

Hyksos A group of people from
Asia who invaded Egypt
c.1670 BC.

Inundation The annual flooding
of the Nile River.

Mummy The preserved body of
an Ancient Egyptian.

Nome Administrative district of
Ancient Egypt, ruled on behalf of
the king by a nomarch.

Papyrus Parchment made from
reeds.

Pharaoh Title given to the king
of Egypt.

Pyramid A tomb built for an
Ancient Egyptian king.

Shaduf A device used by
farmers in Ancient Egypt for
raising water from the Nile.

Index

Photographic credits:

Abbreviations: t=top, m=middle, b=bottom, r=right, l=left

The majority of pictures were reproduced by Courtesy of the Trustees of the British Museum apart from the following images – Title page, 5t, 6t, 6–7, 9, 12t, 14t, 14–15, 15r, 16t, 28t, 28b, 29t: Dr. Anne Millard; 4mr: Roger Wood/CORBIS; 14b: Spectrum Colour Library; 15l, 23bl: Robert Harding Picture Library; 28–29: Charles de Vere; 29m: Hutchinson Library; 29b Frank Spooner Pictures.